SURVIVING

Tough Times

Reginald E. Smith

ISBN: 978-0-578-10422-5

Published by UG Publications
Detroit, Michigan 48208
Copyright ©Reginald E. Smith 2012
All rights reserved

Printed in the United States of America
Design by UG Publications

Let's Pray! God, we do come to you for the answer to life's most difficult question and we pray that our faith will sustain us through our most trying times. Strengthen us, we pray. In Jesus' name, Amen!

ATTITUDE AND ACTIONS MATTER
Job Chapter 2

Verse 10: But he said to her, 'You speak as any foolish woman would speak. Shall we receive the good at the hand of God, and not receive the bad?' In all this, Job did not sin with his lips.

How one reacts to a situation says a lot about their faith, integrity and their trust in God. Job was the victim of a demoniac attack and he was innocent of the things that were happening to him. It really was not his fault; but nevertheless, he had to suffer.

Job's situation was so bad that even, Job's wife wanted him to end his suffering by cursing God and then allowing God to kill him. This is the wrong answer to the problems and trials of life. Blaming God and then forsaking Him is only what the devil wants us to do when things are really bad.

Job suffered a long time, but maintained his integrity. His actions matched his beliefs, despite the fact that things had gone from good to bad almost overnight.

Maybe God is considering us, to see how steadfast we will be in times of trouble. Are you currently going through a difficult ordeal? What has been your response? Are you mad as #*@!? Or are you blaming others? Have you stopped attending church? Have you stopped praying? Are you listening to bad advice? Or are you remaining steadfast in your faith? Do you still believe God for a breakthrough?

NOTES

_____

_____

_____

_____

_____

_____

_____

Let's Pray! God, I have been experiencing some rough times, some even terrible times, but I know that you are able to help me through. So, today Lord, I renew my trust in you, believing that you are going to work it out. In Jesus' name, Amen!

WE MUST FIGHT BACK
Job Chapter 3
Verse 11: Why did I not die at birth, come forth from the womb and expire?

Why? Why? Why? I really don't see any need in repeating this question over and over again, unless you are Job. His whole life had been turned upside down and he lost just about everything that meant anything to him, his children, his property, his livestock, his wealth, and his health. Job lamented the very day of his existence, he cursed the day he was born. Job thought that if he had died in the womb, he would not be alive to see this day of trouble.

Death can seem to be a viable option when calamities come upon you and linger. This thought is a demoniac attack upon the mind. We must not give in to such types of thoughts, especially suicidal thoughts. Why? Because where the mind goes, so goes our way of life. If you can begin to take back your way of thinking, and begin to believe that in the midst of trouble and adversity, things are going to work out. Your recovery and your comeback will begin when you make up your mind not to give up, regardless to what had happened or to what was lost.

NOTES

_____

_____

_____

_____

_____

_____

_____

_____

_____

_____

Let's Pray! God, today we come to you because we know that you are able to keep us in perfect peace even when all of the troubles of the world are around us. Give us, we pray, a strong mind to fight those prevailing thoughts of giving up. In Jesus' name, Amen!

ARE YOU ABLE TO HANDLE IT?
Chapter 4 and 5

Verses 4-5: Your words have supported those who were stumbling, and you have made firm the feeble knees. But now it has come to you, and you are impatient; it touches you, and you are dismayed.

Eliphaz accused Job of not practicing what he preached. Job had encouraged others in their times of trouble, but was not heeding his own advise. Eliphaz believed that he had received this information through a vision at night and that Job had sinned and should reach out to God. *How many times have your friends known more about why you are in trouble than you do?* Eliphaz didn't have much faith in the human race and believed that they could not be trusted. He further believes that the godless were born to grieve, and that Job must have sinned. Eliphaz urged Job to take his case before the Lord who is able to turn Job's situation around.

Eliphaz's understanding is called retribution, in that you reap what you sow. This is not true of all of life's troubles; some situations in our lives can be attributed to what was done in the past. Sometimes trouble comes as a result of belonging to a fallen humanity and sometimes things just happen by accident. But, if you know that you have been doing the right things, then hold on to your faith and integrity.

NOTES

_____
_____
_____
_____
_____
_____
_____
_____

Let's pray! God, we have been experiencing some trouble in our lives and we ask that you keep us and sustain us through these difficult times. In Jesus' name, Amen!

FACE THE ACCUSATIONS
Job Chapter 6
Verse 24: Teach me, and I will be silent; make me understand how I have gone wrong.

Job finally spoke and made his case before his friends. First, because of the greatness of his sorrow and all of the trouble he had gone through, Job asked, "don't I have the right to complain?" Sure, every one of us feels a need to complain when trouble comes our way, but should we?

Second, Job wished that God would end his misery and let him die, for death looked better to Job than life. When we have lasting trouble, suicidal thoughts can enter your mind, but this is the work of the enemy who tries to make you think that God has forsaken you or forgotten you, this is not the case.

Third, Job told his friends that they were not reliable and that he cannot depend on them for support or help in his time of need. It is true when we are in trouble our friends are few in number.

Fourth, Job challenged Eliphaz to show Job his guilt. We must stand up for ourselves in the face of false accusation and defend ourselves against the lies of others.

Finally, Job told his friends to stop assuming that he had sinned because bad things have happened. Too often, people wrongly assume the worst before they know the fact.

NOTES

_____

_____

_____

_____

_____

_____

_____

Let's Pray! God in Heaven, please hear our prayer, help us in times of trouble and show us how to speak to those in need, so that your name may be glorified. In Jesus' name, Amen!

TRUST GOD WHEN YOU CANNOT TRACE HIM
Job Chapter 7

Verse 5: My flesh is clothed with worms and dirt; my skin hardens, and then breaks out again.

Job's troubles lasted longer than what he had thought he could bear. He was without much of an explanation as to why "he had become the target of God?" He knew God had allowed this to happen to him, but he was unsure as to why he had to go through all of this suffering, both physical and emotional.

We all have situations and circumstances that make us wonder whether or not God cares about us, or whether God even knows that we are in trouble or suffering. When you reach these moments in your life, where there seems to be no explanation for your trouble and pain, remember you must trust God even when you cannot trace him.

To trust is to believe in God's word despite the current circumstance we face. Remember trouble exists in a fallen humanity, but know that our God is ever present and our faith is key in times of trials and trouble.

NOTES

_____

_____

_____

_____

_____

_____

_____

_____

_____

_____

_____

Let's Pray! God, we know that you are a caring and loving God and that you will see us through our most difficult days, so we trust in you. In Jesus' name, Amen!

GOD RESTORES US
Job Chapter 8
Verse 6: If you are pure and upright, surely then he will rouse himself for you and restore to you your rightful place.

The assault on Job continued as another of Job's friends spoke about Job's guilt and the need for Job to admit that he had sinned before the Almighty God. Job's friends operated out of a retribution theology, in that "you reap what you sow". Meaning, if Job was innocent, he would not have suffered because only the unrighteous suffer.

We know that this is not always the case; in fact, sometimes the unrighteous seem blessed and the righteous continue to suffer.

Judaism has a clear understanding of, obey God and be blessed and disobey God and be cursed. But what happens when the righteous are suffering at no fault of theirs and the unrighteous continue in their lives as normal?

Bildad, the Shuhite, was correct in understanding that God restores us. Bildad said in verse 7, "though your beginning was small, your latter days will be very great". No matter where you stand on the matter, Our God has the power to make your "latter days" very great. I believe that if we continue to trust in God, and his word, our worst days will become our best days, so, don't worry. God knows how to turn your situation around.

NOTES

_____

_____

_____

_____

_____

_____

_____

Let's Pray! God in Heaven, we do acknowledge you as the only one who can make a bad situation better and a better situation the best, so we surrender to both your will and your way. In Jesus' name, Amen!

TAKE YOUR ISSUE DIRECTLY TO GOD
Job Chapter 9
Verse 4: He is wise in heart, and mighty in strength
—who has resisted him, and succeeded? —

Job knew that no human can stand up against God, and even though we may not understand what or why we are going through things, Job fully understood that it was foolish to try to contend with God. God has the power to destroy both the wicked and the righteous, if he so chooses.

Job requested that there be a mediator between God and man; and for us there is, Jesus Christ, our mediator! He is the only one who can make our case and then solve our case. During this period Christ had not yet come, but now we can take all of our concerns in prayer to God through our Lord and Savior Jesus Christ. *Thank you God that we can now go boldly before the throne of Grace and find help in our times of trouble.*

Job had to try to defend himself in the midst of accusations but our defense is found in and through Jesus Christ and the Holy Spirit, our advocate. Whatever you are facing and don't understand, take your case, not to your friends and family, but take it straight to our heavenly Father, because your mediator is waiting on you to pray!

NOTES

_____

_____

_____

_____

_____

_____

Let's Pray! God, now that we understand that you are waiting to help us and give us the hope we need in trying times, we surrender our situation to you this day. In Jesus' name, Amen!

FIGHT WITH YOUR FAITH
Job Chapter 10
*Verse 12: You have granted me life and steadfast love,
and your care has preserved my spirit*

Job was depressed as he began to blame God for all of the troubles he experienced in his life. Job knew God had the power to deliver him from his misery but in Job's mind, God would not, and this in and of itself drove Job into deep despair.

Depression slowly takes over ones moods and emotional stability. You wake up one day and you don't feel like getting out of bed, and you don't have the energy to do anything, and you could care less about what is happening in the world around you. You live in the ferris wheel of life; your life goes around and around not going anywhere.

Maybe you are depressed or you know someone who is constantly depressed and without answers to the question of why are you going through what you are going through. Well, depression is serious and should not be taken lightly and must be attended to by doctors, and other professionals but it must also be attended to and addressed by the person them self. You have to fight the fight with your faith, and with the Word. Know if you got into it you can get out of it.

NOTES

Let's Pray! Dear God, we ask that you help us through our state of despair and deliver us to the victory that is in Jesus Christ we pray. Amen!

LET GOD VINDICATE YOU
Job Chapter 11

Verse 4: For you say, "My conduct is pure, and I am clean in God's* sight."*

Job's third friend finally spoke to the heart of the matter that, God was punishing Job less than what he deserved. *Ouch, that hurts, you mean that Job's punishment should be worst than what he had already experienced, well according to Zophar, yes.* He further stated that Job cannot comprehend the ways of God, and that if he confessed his sins he would find hope. Everyone in trouble wants to get out no matter how they got into trouble and the friends of Job used their best understanding to try to help end Job's trouble.

However, they didn't understand everything involved and that is why they spoke to him the way they did. They were trying to help him and move him into a better situation, but when you know you are living right and have been walking right in the sight of God, all you have to do is hold onto your integrity. This may come across as being stubborn to some and arrogant to others but hold on anyway and let God vindicate you.

NOTES

_____
_____
_____
_____
_____
_____
_____
_____
_____
_____
_____

Let's Pray! God, we have no one to trust but you and no one fully understands but you, so God we pray that you help us to hold on to what is right and let go of anything that is not right in your sight we pray, in Jesus' name. Amen!

GOD IS IN CONTROL
Job Chapter 12
*Verse 10: In his hand is the life of every living thing
and the breath of every human being.*

Job could not remain silent when Zophar the know-it-all spoke. Job said that even animal and plant life know the things that Zophar has claimed to know, and that is why, sometimes, God allows the wicked to scoff at the good. Job spoke about the omniscient and omnipotent God and that God is in control of everything that happens.

God doesn't get worried about the bad economy, the wars in the land, or even people who seem to be out of control. God has control over human history, even though he doesn't control every event in our lives. He is in control over the outcome of the human race and will through time guide the events to line up with his will for us. Now, it is best that we trust in God for the best outcome in our lives. We must allow the Holy Spirit to speak to us about what is happening in our lives and guide us according to the word and the will of God.

NOTES

_____

_____

_____

_____

_____

_____

_____

_____

_____

_____

_____

Let's Pray! Dear God, we who are your children come to you today asking that you show us the way we are to live and if we are off course in our life please return us to the right path. We pray, in Jesus' name. Amen!

LISTEN RATHER THAN ACCUSE
Job Chapter 13
Verse 5: If you would only keep silent, that would be your wisdom!

"If you would only keep silent that would be your wisdom!" Those were the words of Job because Job knew that everybody speaking was not speaking for God. Job was saying listen rather than accuse and what wonderful advice to us who have friends that are in trouble and are having a difficult time. *Friends should learn to listen, this is 90% of the help and the other 10% is godly advice.*

Job wanted God to stop terrifying him with His awesome presence and he wanted the bitterness of God to stop, because he felt as if God had been accusing him of some sin. Now here is the key, Job maintained his integrity throughout this chapter holding on to the idea that he had committed no sin, and that he had walked upright in the sight of God.

When you know you have done no wrong, which is not the case with most of us. You can take your case to God in prayer and through the blood of Jesus receive at least a hearing in the sight of Almighty God.

NOTES

_____

_____

_____

_____

_____

_____

_____

_____

_____

_____

Let's Pray! God in heaven, we need some answers to the things that are not happening and some of the things that have happened in our lives. Show us the way! We pray in Jesus' name Amen!

MY LIFE WAS INTENDED TO BE A GREAT EXPERIENCE
Job Chapter 14
Verse 1: A mortal, born of woman, few of days and full of trouble,

Job raised interesting ideas all of which we would not agree with today, but for his time the theology of life and death was developing. The first thing Job said, was "a mortal (person), born of a woman, few of days and full of trouble," while life can be short for some it is not always full of trouble. We should not adopt this idea of Job as being universal in scope.

Yes, there is trouble in the world and will always be some form of trouble but the Bible declares further that God delivers the righteous out of it all. We can not allow Job's assessment of his trouble to become the theology by which we live. Life was intended by God to be a great experience not just a painful, drama filled experience.

So, if you are experiencing trouble after trouble after trouble, it's time to begin to claim victory, and a better life for you and your family. When we don't deny our troubles we solve them and move on, so take your life back from despair and trouble and begin to live the life God intended for you to live; a life in his presence and full of joy.

NOTES

_____
_____
_____
_____
_____
_____
_____

Let's Pray! God trouble has invaded our life and now God we ask that you guide us out of a trouble filled life and into your perfect will, where we can experience the fullness of joy in Jesus' name, Amen!

EXPECT A SECOND ATTACK
Job Chapter 15
Verse 2: Should the wise answer with windy knowledge, and fill themselves with the east wind?

Eliphaz began with another round of rebuke for Job, in that he told Job he was nothing but a bag of wind and that Job was acting like a wise man when really he was a foolish man. Eliphaz insisted that sinful people suffer and that Job was a sinful person. Eliphaz spent the entire chapter telling how sinful people suffer.

Now, while all what Eliphaz said was true, what he assumed about Job was not true. A lot of times people make assumptions about us that are simply not true. What happens when you are the victim of accusations that are simply not true, it takes a lot of patience to listen to false claims without losing your cool. The world in which we live in is not simply, "the unrighteous suffer, and the righteous are blessed." So, while following God can lead to overflowing blessing we must also learn how to deal with difficult times. It's during the difficult times when we need people around us who are encouraging us and keeping us in the right frame of mind, so that we simply just don't lose it.

NOTES

_____

_____

_____

_____

_____

_____

_____

_____

Let's pray! God we know that you have the best life planned for us. But right now we are experiencing some tough times that we thought would be over by now. Please God, give us the day to day strength we need to endure in Jesus' name Amen!

WALK A MILE IN MY SHOES
Job Chapter 16
Verse 4: I also could talk as you do, if you were in my place; I could join words together against you, and shake my head at you.

Job responded to his three friends who had accused him of all kinds of sins and wrongdoing. *It can be easier to give advice than it is to take advice, and it is easier to condemn others than to be condemned.*

Sometimes, you reach your boiling point and you have taken all you can take from people who are not in your shoes, and who do not understand your situation or where you are coming from, or how you got in the current situation. Thank God, that we have a Savior who understands the human experience has walked more than a mile in the human drama, can identify with us and knows what it is to be forsaken, lied on, and totally rejected.

Despite all that he endured, he stayed faithful to his assignment and mission to the end. So, let us look not to Job but to Jesus who is the author and finisher of our faith. For it is in him we live and have our existence.

NOTES

_____

_____

_____

_____

_____

_____

_____

_____

_____

_____

Let's pray! God we do thank you that you understand what we have been through and what we are currently facing in our lives even at this very moment, so God thank you for just understanding and caring for us no matter what we are currently going through, in Jesus' name, we pray Amen!

LOOK TO GOD
Job Chapter 17

Verse 9: Yet the righteous hold to their way, and they that have clean hands grow stronger and stronger.

Job looked to God to defend him in this chapter and when you cannot defend yourself that's the best place to look. God knows even though God may not have revealed all to us, he knows, and with those words we can find some comfort in just about any situation. Place your trust in the fact that God knows and cares for you and yours.

Job's hope had disappeared and he looked forward to death and to dying because he believed he would find comfort in death itself. No human can judge him for the way he feels because not many people can totally identify with everything that Job has gone through in his life.

Despair is funny, in that it can totally rob you of all hope. If you are at this point and you feel that death is the answer. Wait! This is just one chapter of your life with many more to go, and if you give up in the middle, you will never see the end. Remember, God knows and cares just for you even when it doesn't feel like no one else cares.

NOTES

_____

_____

_____

_____

_____

_____

_____

_____

_____

Let's pray! Dear God, we come to you at a low point in our lives. So low that we can no longer look up. We do know that you care for us and that you are right there even in our most trying and difficult time. Renew our hope in you. In Jesus' name, Amen!

SUFFERING WHILE UNDER ATTACK
Job Chapter 18

Verse 4: You who tear yourself in your anger— shall the earth be forsaken because of you, or the rock be removed out of its place?

A second round of attacks by Job's friend began as Bildad laid out his case that disease is the firstborn of death. Wow! This is one way to make a person feel worse while suffering from the loss of his children, the loss of his wealth, and who had a diseased body. The devil destroyed everything he was allowed to touch. This is how the enemy will work in your life as well as mind, if allowed he will destroy, disturb, and disrupt any and all areas of our life. The devil even uses the weak around us to attack us with lies, gossip, and insults of all kind. Bildad thought he was helping, in fact he added to the pain and torment of Job.

There are times when we need friends to lead us out of denial and into the truth of God's Word, because we can all, at times, walk in the darkness of stubbornness and self-interest, with no regard for God and his written or spoken word. Be encouraged to keep fighting the good fight of faith no matter the situation, and no matter what you have been through, faith in God works! Death is coming, but so is our Lord, Jesus Christ. Be ready by placing one's trust in Christ as your Savior and Lord, from the penalty of sin, which is death.

NOTES

_____

_____

_____

_____

_____

_____

_____

Let's pray! God, when death arrives, whether early in my life, late in my life, or somewhere in between, I want to be secure in my walk with you. Come into my life Lord Jesus, I repent of my sins and I accept you as my Lord and Savior, in Jesus' name, Amen!

HOPE IN A CRISIS
Job Chapter 19
Verses 25: For I know that my Redeemer lives, and that at the last he* will stand upon the earth;*

How do you continue to make it day in and day out without any change in your current situation? Job asked it this way, "How long will you torment me, and break me in pieces with words?"

No matter what people may say, words hurt, the way people speak to us, and the things they say to us, it all hurts, and sometimes the pain can last a lifetime. Maybe you have been hurt by the words of family, spouse, children, or friends, or even people you work with or worship with, this can be a most devastating time in your life.

But, there is healing for your soul. Job stated in verse 25, "For I know that my Redeemer lives, and that at the last he will stand upon the earth." Those words of hope and assurance came as a result of the early morning devotions and prayer that Job had before the calamities struck his life.

And Job's example should be followed by us. If your life is fine then this is a good day to make a deposit in the well of life, for you never know when you will have to make a withdrawal on the worst day of your life. If you are in a crisis be assured, and keep the faith like Job, knowing that our redeemer, the one who can restore all, lives and will be standing at the end of time.

NOTES

_____

_____

_____

_____

_____

_____

Let's pray! Dear God, thank you, you will outlast any trouble that we could ever experience on this earth, and thank you for reminding us, that in the end we win in Jesus' name, Amen!

PAY ATTENTION
Job Chapter 20

Verse 2: Pay attention! My thoughts urge me to answer, because of the agitation within me.

Have you ever insulted anyone? Well, this is what Zophar felt Job had done to him, insulted his intelligence, and hurt his pride, because of the rebuke that Job gave in the earlier chapters. Zophar felt that he had explained Job's suffering and helped his friend to regain his senses and he got a stern rebuke in return. So, Zophar did what any good friend would, he fired back at Job with his own rebuke, and restated that the wicked received just retribution for their actions, and that the fate of the wicked will run into the "fierce anger" of God. Zophar was right, the wicked will perish, and the righteous of God will prevail, but to associate Job's suffering with the way of the wicked was going too far.

Some people will not stand up for themselves but, what about standing on the Word of God, and not backing down. Standing up for yourself is important but what you stand upon is more important. The Bible tells us in Isaiah, "that the grass withers, and the flowers fade, but the Word of God will stand forever." Zophar said at the beginning of this chapter "Pay Attention!" not to what others are saying about you but what God has already said about you, so stand up for yourself just make sure it's upon the Word of God.

NOTES

_____

_____

_____

_____

_____

_____

_____

Let's Pray! Dear God we are often afraid to stand up for ourselves, but we now know that we can stand firm upon your word. Thank you, for the strength that comes from your word. In Jesus' name, Amen!

WE WALK BY OUR FAITH & TOTAL TRUST IN GOD
Job Chapter 21

Verse 7: Why do the wicked live on, reach old age, and grow mighty in power?

What a day? What a day? We never know what a day will bring, how it will turn-out or what it will turn up. Sometimes, we have questions about one day in our lives but Job questioned his entire life and the life of those without regard for God or the things of God.

People of God, hear me, we must fight the good fight of faith, and not give-in or give-up despite tough times or tight situations. The enemy is on the rise and is trying to convince the people of God, that the fight cannot be won, that there is no use in trying. If you feel sorry about your situation or are down on yourself, get up and get back into the fight.

Despite what we see, we walk by our faith and total trust in God, to guide us and guard us. So, people have disappointed you fight the good fight of faith. Fight for what you know God has for you. The Bible says the meek will inherit the earth, not the weak. Meek means to be humble, humble means to stay in your God-given assignment. Like Jesus, our Savior and Lord, who stayed on the cross and died to pay the price for our Salvation. Thank God, for those who, despite their misery fight back against the enemy for justice.

NOTES

_____

_____

_____

_____

_____

_____

Let's Pray! Lord, despite what it looks like, we are in the race not only to finish, but to win. Put the wind to our backs and victory in front of us, in Jesus' name, Amen!

IT'S YOUR LIFE
Job Chapter 22
Verse 8: The powerful possess the land, and the favored live in it.

Job's friends spoke directly to his face. As hard core as the words of Eliphaz sounded, at least he spoke directly to Job. Eliphaz thought he was right and he laid it all out on the line. He accused Job of all kinds of wrongdoings that he believed Job was guilty of and that may have caused all of the trouble in Job's life. Eliphaz didn't believe that God had much regard for human's righteousness and Job who claimed to be, not guilty, was the worst of all sinners. Deep down all of Job's friends believed if he would admit his wrongdoing and everything would go away.

Your life is in your hand. You must do something with your life or others will do it for you. Many people get into trouble because they assume they know what others are saying about them and what others thinking about them. When was the last time you had people, tell you to your face, what they think about you and your situation without, being personally angry at you? Maybe you are the person who thinks they know what is going on in the lives of your fiends and family and you have placed yourself in the seat of Judgment.

NOTES

_____
_____
_____
_____
_____
_____
_____
_____

Let's Pray! Dear God in heaven above, which is your throne and earth is your footstool. I repent of my judgmental attitude towards others and ask that you help me not to condemn those you are saved with your precious blood. In Jesus' name, Amen!

WE PRAY
Job Chapter 23
Verse 3: O that I knew where I might find him that I might come even to his dwelling!

Job felt abandoned by God and everyone. Where is God when you need him most? Where is he in your time of trouble? Why hasn't he answered? You feel despair and disbelief because the God of creation sometimes feels absent at our most pressing times. These questions and concerns are on the hearts and minds of many when they are in a time of crisis.

How do we get closer to God in times of trouble? Well the answer is simpler than you think. We pray, we pray, we pray, and we pray.

God knows the language of prayer from his children. Jesus said in the Gospel, "My sheep hear my voice, and another they will not follow." These words are important.

Job had done a lot of talking, to his friends and within himself, but he had not prayed. He had not listened to the Shepherd's voice. Despair makes us not want to pray but we must pray anyway. You have to have a conversation with God as you ride in your car, lie in your bed, or sit at your desk. It doesn't matter where you have the conversation as long as you are talking with God; you gain understanding and move into appropriate action.

NOTES

Let's Pray! Dear God, we sometimes do not talk to you when we feel despair, depression or hopelessness. We ask that you keep prayer before us at all times because we know that you are waiting and listening for our prayers, in Jesus' name, Amen.

NOT OF THE WORLD
Job Chapter 24

Verse 22: Yet God˙ prolongs the life of the mighty by his power; they rise up when they despair of life.

Sometimes you see things happening that are wrong, sometimes you know people who are behaving poorly and you wonder how they can get away with such wrongful acts. At the same time, you are trying to do the right thing, live right in the sight of Almighty God, and do the things that you know you need to do in your life and for your family, while others seem to be getting ahead of you in life. Job wanted to know, why was it that all of the wicked of his time seemed to get away with evil acts? How was it that they seemed to go unpunished?

Many times the world in which we live seems unfair and out of balance. Our observations are correct and real. The reasons the Bible gives for such lopsidedness is because of sin and the fallen nature of humanity. All of us are prone to sin, and become deceivers, liars and cheats, to name a few of the ways of fallen man. However, God knows that this is not the end because God does have the last say-so and in the end the ways of God will win out.

In the meantime, we must strive to bring about the will of God in the sphere of life that we control or influence. This is why Jesus taught us to pray "your will be done on earth as it is in heaven."

NOTES

_____

_____

_____

_____

_____

_____

_____

This is the prayer we must say on this day, in this hour and in this time, "Your will be done on earth this very day", in Jesus' name, Amen!

WE MUST HAVE A RELATIONSHIP WITH GOD
Job Chapter 25

Verse 2:'Dominion and fear are with God;' he makes peace in his high heaven.

We all, at times, wrestle with our understanding of God. Bildad made his final argument against Job and raised the question of how can human beings be righteous in the sight of God? This question has merit because being right in God's standard is conforming to the ways of God; it's having God's approval on your life. Bildad argued that Job or no one else can be righteous in the sight of God.

No matter how good we think we have been or how good we have been, our righteousness is still not sufficient for God. This is why having Christ as your personal Savior is essential, and having a personal relationship with God through prayer and worship goes without question, and why belonging to a fellowship of believers is important. It keeps bringing us back to center, whenever we get off course. Remember our righteousness is connected with our relationship we have in Jesus and not how well, we have lived.

NOTES

_____
_____
_____
_____
_____
_____
_____
_____
_____
_____
_____

Let's Pray! Dear God, who brings us all into a right standing, we surrender our will and our lives to you this day, so that nothing can stand between us. Keep us we pray, in Jesus' name Amen!

BELIEVE IN THE POWER OF GOD
Job Chapter 26
Verse 12: By his power he stilled the Sea; by his understanding he struck down Rahab.

Job had not lost his fire or his ability to keep up with the criticism of his friends; he told them that he had not been helped at all by their comments.

Sometimes we have to let the people around us know that they are not helping with their criticisms and that they are adding to the problems we already have to face in our own lives. Lift up your head, keep fighting back and don't let people walk all over you, because you are made in the image of God and after his likeness. You have to remain strong by relying on the Word of God in tough times. Attending weekly worship, reading the Bible daily and praying is essential for maintaining strength during hard times.

Job never doubted the power of God. Job spoke about the mighty power of God and how the creation of the universe is but a small example of God's power. He meant that, what our eyes behold, the stars and moon we see at night, the sun that rises and sets in the horizons are but a small part of the power of God. Think about the faith that Job had after all he had gone through. What kind of faith in God do you have after your ordeal?

NOTES

_____

_____

_____

_____

_____

_____

_____

Let's Pray! Dear God, times have been tough but we realize that you have power over the world and power over our lives. Take us to the next level of trust in you, where we believe even when we cannot understand, in Jesus' name, Amen!

LIVE RIGHT
Job Chapter 27

Verse 8: For what is the hope of the godless when God cuts them off, when God takes away their lives?

Job's situation was far from just a rough week or a couple of bad days, his whole world had been turned upside down and all he had and loved was almost gone. Job verses 3, 4, and 5 state "as long as my breath is in me and the spirit of God is in my nostrils, my lips will not speak falsehood, and my tongue will not utter deceit. Far be it from me to say that you are right; until I die I will not put away my integrity from me." Stop claiming to know God on Sunday morning and then living as if you never met God throughout your work week.

God wants people of integrity, meaning people who are upright and who strive to live right in all of their dealings. You may not have all of the money you want, but God wants you to handle what you have in the right way. You may not have had all of the benefits of others, but God wants you to live the best you can with what you have. People make excuses as to why they do the things they do, why they tell the lies they tell or why they carry out the actions that they know are wrong from the get-go. God wants people who will hold on to the truth and will live their lives without deceit, dishonesty, and deception.

NOTES

_____

_____

_____

_____

_____

_____

_____

Let's Pray! Dear God, who is our righteousness we come to you thanking you for the example of Job's life which demonstrated that despite what we are going through we can still live right in your sight, in Jesus' name, Amen!

WISDOM IS ESSENTIAL
Job Chapter 28
Verse 12:'But where shall wisdom be found? And where is the place of understanding?

The key to a better life is wisdom. Wisdom is making the right choices in life; it is having an understanding about the things that make for a better life. The search for wisdom is most essential, because its value is greater than all of the gold and silver in the world.

If you, throughout your life are choosing the right paths to follow, you will always be in the places you are suppose to be in and you will receive the things this particular path has for you. Making the right decisions are key. Many people suffer because they lack insight, and the understanding needed in certain situations. How many "missed opportunities" have you had because you were busy doing the wrong thing? How many people have you allowed to stay in your path because you were too afraid to let them go?

The wisdom of which Job spoke about comes from God, and God alone. This is why we seek God's will in every decision we make. Seeking the wisdom of God builds our relationship with our heavenly Father, and draws us closer to God each and every day.

NOTES

Let's Pray! Dear God, grant us the wisdom we need to make the right choices in our everyday life! So, that we will always be in the right place at the right time doing the right things, in Jesus' name, Amen!

REFLECT ON LIFE
Job Chapter 29

[2] *Verse 2:'O that I were as in the months of old, as in the days when God watched over me;*

It is good to be able to think back over life. Job for the first time mentioned the loss of his children and how he missed them. Also, how he helped those in need and how he was respected among the people of his day.

If you have lost in your life and you are now in a stage of depression, or regret, take a little time to think back over the goodness of the Lord, and all of the things he has allowed for you to have and do in your life. Thank God for the good and the bad, but especially the good, even the things you took for granted that are no longer here or the people who are no longer in your life. Remember, what Job has taught us already, "that the Lord gives and the Lord takes away blessed be the name of the Lord".

NOTES

_____
_____
_____
_____
_____
_____
_____
_____
_____
_____
_____
_____
_____
_____
_____

Let's Pray! Dear God we do thank you for all that you have blessed us with. We thank you for the memories that we have left and all that you have allowed us to experience in our lives, in Jesus' name, Amen!

MAINTAIN SPIRITUAL SANITY
Job Chapter 30

Verse 26: But when I looked for good, evil came; and when I waited for light, darkness came.

What happens when your world is turned upside down and the very people that once looked to you for help now look down on you? The places where you were the most respected are now the very places where you are despised the most?

Our world can be turned upside down in just a matter of moments, with just a phone call to say that a loved one has just died, that our home has been broken into, that this is our last day on the job, or we find out the one we love has been cheating on us and lying to us.

Usually, it doesn't take much for most of us to lose control, but for Job it took a lot for an extensive period of time. God was at fault for all of the misery that Job experienced and Job no longer hid this fact from anyone. He felt that the Lord had allowed all of this misery to come upon him. Job said in verse 21, "You have turned cruel to me; with the might of your hand you persecute me." This was a clear indication that he came to blame God for all of his troubles.

If trouble without the hope of solutions lasts too long we may all break down and lose it, no wonder we have to continue to feed our faith, throughout our lives, and that daily devotion is essential for spiritual sanity.

NOTES

_____
_____
_____
_____
_____

Let's Pray! Dear God, teach us in the hours of our uncertainty, what we must do and how we must approach the changed situations in our lives, in Jesus' name, Amen!

SUFFERING FOR NO REASON
Job Chapter 31
Verse 4: Does he not see my ways, and number all my steps?

Job ended his case for justice and retribution by stating all of the reasons why he would be guilty if he had done a specific thing and he named them one by one. Job in his finest hour laid out the reasons why or why not he should suffer for the sins he had been accused of. Throughout this chapter he presented his case not only before others but before the Lord.

Suffering happens to all of us in one form or another. Sometimes, we just don't understand what we are going through or why we are going through certain things in our lives. Sometimes we know exactly why we are going through our tough times. For example, if we don't pay our tithes & offering then we can expect devourers to come and eat up our financial opportunities, or we have wronged others and are reaping the consequences of our actions, or we have neglected our responsibilities and now the situation has worsened.

These examples are some of the reasons why we go through the things we do, but for all the time Job had no clue and had no understanding as to why he suffered. If you feel like you are in a similar situation then lay out your case before the Lord in prayer.

NOTES

_____

_____

_____

_____

_____

_____

_____

Let's Pray! God sometimes we face things and have to go all the way through them without an understanding or explanation as to why these things are happening to us. Please, we pray, keep us even in our darkest hour, in Jesus' name, Amen!

BE WISE
Job Chapter 32

Verse 1: So these three men ceased to answer Job, because he was righteous in his own eyes.

Sometimes silence is golden, and we should all learn when to speak. We do not assume that just because he spoke to us early in the morning that he will do the same the next morning. If you are heavily involved in the church, or in the ministry itself in some form be it a minister, deacon, leader in the local church, you sometimes have to invoke the rule of silence so that you will not speak out of turn, or ahead of God.

Elihu was the youngest but he displayed the most wisdom of all of the men, including Job himself. Proving that wisdom is not confined to a specific age nor is it naturally granted at a particular age. Wisdom is sometimes elusive and slippery and avoids those who think they already have the answered. Elihu was never mentioned as being around until he spoke in this chapter. During this time it was respectful for the younger men to wait their turn to speak in any situation where their elders were gathered.

When was the last time you sat in silence among your elders and listened to the conversation of the sage around you? God knows that not all of your elders display the wisdom of God but there are some, within your circle of influence who have much to say if we would take the time to listen.

NOTES

_____

_____

_____

_____

_____

Let's Pray! Dear God help us to hold our tongue until the right time to speak and sit us around those who are wise in the wisdom of God that we may gain insight in Jesus' name, we pray, Amen!

RECOGNIZE GOD
Job Chapter 33
Verse 14: For God speaks in one way, and in two, though people do not perceive it.

Here, Elihu wanted to educate Job on the justice of God. The friends of Job had spent an enormous amount of time trying to get him to confess his wrongdoing and to admit his sins before God. Elihu did not leave this course of action but added an interesting twist. He admitted his wrongs and spoke of how God gets us back on track when we stray.

We can learn from those around us and we should seek advice when we are making a decision in our life. The Bible declares that there is wisdom in a multitude of counselors. So, if you are in a jam or are making a major decision, seek counsel.

Notably, Elihu was right in one regard, God does speak to his people through dreams and visions often warning them of the dangers or troubles. We must be able to hear the voice of God and to respond appropriately. Many times we are too busy doing things that do not help us move toward our God-given purposes.

Is God warning you or trying to tell you do something? Do you know how the Lord speaks to you? Are you familiar with the ways of God, or do you recognize when it is the Lord is speaking?

NOTES

_____

_____

_____

_____

_____

_____

Let's Pray! Dear God, we come asking that you teach us your ways, help us to recognize how and when you speak to us so we may follow your ways. In Jesus' name, Amen!

OPINION IS NOT GOSPEL
Job Chapter 34
Verse 10: 'Therefore, hear me, you who have sense far be it from God that he should do wickedness, and from the Almighty' that he should do wrong.

What else is there to say when you have said it all, sometimes you get sick of hearing the same thing over and over again, this is where Job is right about now. Elihu picked up where the other friends left off, he accused Job of wrongdoing while making sure he reminded Job of the justice of God.

One may agree with Elihu that God is a just God and that all of his ways are pure, but one cannot help but wonder what was God thinking? There was a lot of talk about him, and God had not said a word.

Sometimes we think we speak for God, and we don't. This is why preaching and ministering has a careful process of discerning the will of God. *The Gospel is the proclamation of the good news of Jesus Christ, and those who preach are really making known what God has said, not coming up with their own ideas of what they think.*

The lesson here is, don't be wise in your own eyes, don't think you have it all together when you don't, and don't become the know-it-all before you check with God. Check out the facts and don't always live in the opinion world. God has a way of getting his word out.

NOTES

_____

_____

_____

_____

_____

_____

_____

Let's Pray! Dear God, keep us from always stating our own opinion as if it is the gospel truth, and help us to speak the truth that comes from your word. In Jesus' name, Amen!

GET INTO ACTION
Job Chapter 35
Verse 13: Surely God does not hear an empty cry, nor does the Almighty regard it.

Elihu continued to hammer Job for his self-righteous ways. He believed that Job had sinned in some way and had spent his time with "empty talk."

I sometimes run into people whom I have not seen for sometime and all they do is talk, talk, and more talk. You have to start walking away or they will talk you to death, about everything and everyone, without realizing how much time has gone by.

Talk can be cheap when it is full of empty promises, plans and ideas that will never see the light of day. Don't become an empty talker, always promising to do something and always planning for some big day without ever doing anything in your life.

Job had a very productive life, but most of the things he had accomplished had been swept away in the troubles of his life. People don't always remember what you have done but they always notice what you are doing now.

Now is all the time you have. So use each day wisely and don't waste your time with a bunch of talk when action is needed and while you could be accomplishing something greater in your life. Are you full of just "empty talk?" Do you always plan but never take action?

NOTES

Let's pray! Dear God of all creation, Redeemer and Savior, we come to you today to ask that you help us get off of the seat of planning and onto the pavement of action. Move us into your will we pray. In Jesus' name, Amen!

TAKE THE LEAD
Job Chapter 36

Verse 5: Surely God is mighty and does not despise any; he is mighty in strength of understanding.

Our God is mighty and his power is unmatched; therefore, we must look to God for all of our concerns and troubles, and we must trust God through all of our situations.

Elihu spoke truth as he defended God before Job and his friends. Elihu knew in whom he believed. This is what makes a difference in our lives, when we can stand up for what we believe in. Life is full of challenges, changes, twist and turns, but we must know what we believe and in whom we believe.

We must live what we profess, because a powerful life is more important than a powerful speech. Sometimes we can say it, but not really live it, and sometimes we know how to speak it, but not walk it. The challenge to any faith is living it daily.

Maybe you are waiting on someone else to lead the way, but once you know the way then you can take the lead yourself. Don't always sit back in the shadows of life waiting for others to take the spiritual lead. God will guide you and protect you as you travel along the way. So my challenge to you is to get off the sidelines and get in the game.

NOTES

Let's pray! Dear God, we must be challenged to take the lead and we must know in whom we believe, so we ask that you clarify our path and strengthen our walk. In Jesus' name, Amen!

CONSIDER GOD'S WORKS
Job Chapter 37
Verse 5: God thunders wondrously with his voice; he does great things that we cannot comprehend.

Our God is an awesome God and his power and majesty is unmatched throughout all of the earth. This was a wonderfully poetic way Elihu expressed the greatness of God.

Oftentimes, we forget how wonderful the world really is, with all of the bad news that constantly comes through the airways of television radio or internet. Many of us get caught up in the everyday routine of life.

We sometimes forget that the world in which we live is truly amazing. The world offers us changing of the seasons, birds of the air, fish of the sea, and land with breathtaking views. If you have not had a chance to visit other parts of the country or the world, I strongly suggest you do, before it is too late.

Don't spend all of your time working or waiting to retire, visit the great creations of God. You will gain a new perspective, and you will greatly appreciate the world in which you live. Remember, that old saying, "travel broadens your horizon." Well it's true, and here is another, "traveling helps you to see how awesome the God you serve really is." I like one line that Elihu gave in verse 14, "Hear this, O Job; stop and consider the wondrous works of God."

NOTES

Let's pray! God we do thank you for this place to live, called Earth, and we appreciate your creation each and every day. Thanks or thinking of us even before we were here. In Jesus' name, Amen!

THE LORD WILL SPEAK
Job Chapter 38

Verses: 1-3: Then the LORD answered Job out of the whirlwind: Who is this that darkens counsel by words without knowledge? Gird up your loins like a man, I will question you, and you shall declare to me.

God finally answered Job, not with answers, but with more questions. God speaks when we finish speaking and getting the opinions of others. God speaks when we have run through our discourse, and have expounded on all of our theories and ideas. God speaks when we finish explaining what we think about our situation. God speaks when all of the advice of our friends and family has been heard, and we have finished searching our heart and mind for the-all-to allusive answers.

God speaks--when we shut-up. I have found this principle to be true throughout my life and maybe you have experienced the same. Here, Job had come to the end of his inquiries, and so had all of his friends, and then God spoke. I want you to notice that God asked a series of questions about the earth, the oceans, light, snow and rain, and the stars, to which Job or no other human is able to answer, in full.

I believe the lesson in all of this is, don't be a know-it-all. None of us have the answers to life's most challenging questions. So let us surrender our knowledge to the all-knowing God, give up our quest for answers and seek the Lord, and God of faith.

NOTES

_____

_____

_____

_____

_____

_____

Let's Pray! Dear God, thank you for speaking to us in unexpected ways after suffering and dealing with long lasting difficult situations. Thank you, for being the God of our creation and the redeemer of our soul. In Jesus' name, Amen!

LISTEN TO THE GOD
Job Chapter 39

Verse 27: Is it at your command that the eagle mounts up and makes its nest on high?

Finally, God is speaking, and when the Lord is speaking, let all of the earth keep silent before him. Being able to hear from God is a good place to be, because when we have not heard from God, we move in the wrong direction, say the wrong things, be in the wrong place, and do the wrong thing.

If you are in the midst of a tough situation right now then the best thing you can have going for you is to hear clearly from the Lord. Don't take this time for granted because the Lord is speaking and his words are everlasting and will do more for you in the short and long term.

Please take notes on the life of Job. He was a righteous and upright man in all the land, so much so that the Lord bragged before Satan on Job. God was so proud of Job and the way he lived. Now notice how long it was before the Lord answered him or even said one word to Job. Sometimes we hear our own spirit speaking and sometimes we are listening to the voice of others, and even the voice of Satan can sound like God. He knows when we are most needy and in difficult circumstances. So, wherever you are in your life at this time, appreciate the Word of God, the spoken word, the written word, and most of all, the living word which is Christ Jesus.

NOTES

_____

_____

_____

_____

_____

Let's Pray! Dear God
in heaven, we do thank you for
speaking to our heart, in Jesus'
name, Amen!

GOD KNOWS BEST
Job Chapter 40
Verse 2: 'Shall a fault-finder contend with the Almighty?' Anyone who argues with God must respond.'

God knew what Job needed better than Job. Job knew his place and realized that God was still sovereign despite the troubles and heartaches.

Knowing your place with God is as important as knowing God for yourself. If you don't have a personal relationship with God, start a daily devotion, which includes praying and studying God's word.

How you know your place with God? The short answer is to realize that He is your creator, redeemer, and sustainer, for without God you could not exist. People who live their lives without acknowledging God are being deceived by Satan. Others have a casual attitude towards God. These types of mentalities are demoniac and destructive.

God knows you are having a hard time. He sees your trouble, and because he has not saved you from these situations, does not mean that God is not real or that he is unconcerned about you.

We don't have all of the answers, nobody does. We must keep the faith and remain hopeful in all situations. With God all things are possible, even while going through trials and tribulations in your life.

NOTES

_____

_____

_____

_____

_____

_____

_____

Let's Pray! Dear God, we may not always understand why things happen or we may not always have the answers. We may not be able to explain the events in our lives, but we still have faith and trust in you. We believe that you are working everything out for our good.

In Jesus' name, Amen!

GOD IS IN CONTROL
Job Chapter 41
Verse 10: No one is fierce enough to rouse him. Who then is able to stand against me?

The Lord our God is the ruler of the heavens and the earth and he knows everything that is going on in his creation. The Leviathan was a sea-monster that personifies chaos, and that is why the Lord talked in this chapter about chaos. He knew tribulation and trouble could come all at once and lead to us losing our faith and trust.

However, for the Lord God, chaos is nothing but a play thing to which the Lord has complete control. The sea, in Job's day, represented chaos and what job experienced is days full of trouble. Here is what God is saying, to you and to me, although our days of trouble may seem overwhelming to us and as if we will not make it through, remember the Lord God has it all in control.

Now, we are going to have to place our complete trust in the Lord as we move forward. We are going to have to believe even when we cannot see that the Lord God will be there for us all the way.

NOTES

_____

_____

_____

_____

_____

_____

_____

_____

_____

_____

Let's pray! Dear God, when our day of trouble comes, help us to lean and trust in you and believe you despite what may come our way.

In Jesus' name, Amen!

THIS IS IT
Job Chapter 42

Verse 10: And the LORD restored the fortunes of Job when he had prayed for his friends; and the LORD gave Job twice as much as he had before.

When God finally speaks, *that is it.* Notice how God started with repentance, then reconciliation and finally restoration.

The Lord God made the friends of Job repent for their sins, thinking that they spoke for the Lord God. Then he made Job pray for them in order for them to get forgiveness and in order for Job to get restoration.

Keep your eyes on the process of God, because it's working even today in our situations. God will not move towards restoration until repentance and reconciliation have happened first. If you are in need of restoration then you need to first make sure that you have turned to God in repentance. Be sure that you have restored those who are in relationship with you, and that you have done all that is required of the Lord God.

Well, *this is it*, and if you need the Lord to move on your behalf; are you trusting him in your day of trouble? Are you holding on to your integrity in the midst of a chaotic situation? Then, I know that the Lord will see you through.

NOTES

Let's Pray. Dear God, Thank you for helping me to survive the tough times in my life. I know that you are with me and that with you I can make it. In Jesus' name, Amen!